RODEO
COLORING BOOK

STEVEN JAMES PETRUCCIO

DOVER PUBLICATIONS
Garden City, New York

INTRODUCTION

American rodeos (from a Spanish word meaning "to surround") have their roots in the late 1700s and early 1800s when Spain controlled much of the American West. Spanish cowboys (called *vaqueros*) helped raise cattle on vast *ranchos*. Annual roundups and branding events soon became occasions for cowboys to demonstrate their skills. Eventually, the Spanish cowboys passed on their skills of horsemanship and roping to American cowboys.

At stockyards, horse shows, and roundup camps across the West, spectators began to gather to watch the cowboys show off their riding and roping talents. Before long, showmen like Buffalo Bill turned these displays into a business. As years passed, rodeo events became standardized to include bareback riding, steer wrestling, team roping, saddle bronc riding, calf roping, and bull riding. In addition, rules and safety regulations were instituted for the protection of both the riders and the animals.

Today, rodeo is more popular and competitive than ever. Millions of viewers watch rodeo on cable TV, not to mention the hundreds of thousands of fans who attend in person. So pick up those crayons, pardner, and get ready for some rodeo coloring fun.

Copyright

Copyright © 2004 by Steven James Petruccio
All rights reserved.

Bibliographical Note

Rodeo Coloring Book is a new work, first published by Dover Publications in 2004.

International Standard Book Number
ISBN-13: 978-0-486-43330-1
ISBN-10: 0-486-43330-7

Manufactured in the United States of America
43330715   2023
www.doverpublications.com

Welcome to the Rodeo. A friendly cowboy clown welcomes one and all to the rodeo!

Opening Parade. The rodeo begins with a grand procession of riders, cowboys, and clowns.

Bareback Bronc Riding. A bareback bronc rider struggles to stay on a furiously bucking horse. This event is often called the most athletic event in rodeo, because the rider has no saddle to sit on, and may only use one hand to hold onto a small rope handle.

Saddle Bronc Riding. Even with a saddle, it's not easy to ride a bucking bronc! The rider must use only one hand on the reins and must stay on for at least eight seconds.

Bull Riding. Look out! Here comes the bull rider out of the chute!

Bull Riding. Bull riding is one of the most exciting events in rodeo. It has also been voted the most dangerous sport in America. The bull rider must hold onto a loosely tied braided rope with only one hand while a furious 1500-pound animal tries to shake him loose.

Rodeo Clown. Rodeo clowns help distract the angry bull after he has thrown the rider, since bulls will often try and attack the rider once he is on the ground.

Barrel Racing. In barrel racing, the premiere event for women rodeo contestants, riders must race around a cloverleaf course marked out with three barrels set up in a triangle. Riders are penalized for any overturned barrels.

Barrel Racing. Whoever returns to the starting gate in the fastest time wins the barrel race!

Trick Roping. Trick ropers perform amazing feats with a lasso. The "Flat Spin" and "Wedding Ring" are two techniques that are the basis for most other trick and fancy roping routines, such as the vertical loop shown here.

Lariat Roping. A skilled roper can perform wonderful tricks with a lariat, including lassoing a rodeo clown before he even knows what's happening.

Cowgirl Breakaway Roping. This is a timed contest in which the contestant must rope a calf and secure the rope to the saddle. Breakaway roping requires perfect coordination between horse and rider. As the roped calf runs forward, time is up when the rope "breaks away" from the saddle.

Team Steer Roping. In this event, one rider (called a "header") must chase down a fast-racing steer, rope him around the neck or horns, and turn the steer to the left. Then his partner (called a "heeler"), tries to rope the steer's hind feet.

Calf Roping. After the calf is given a head start, horse and rider give chase. The cowboy ropes the calf, then jumps from his horse, catches the calf and ties any three of its legs together, using a "pigging string" he carries in his teeth.

Roped and Tied. When the cowboy completes his tie, he throws his hands in the air as a signal to the judge. He then remounts his horse and allows the rope to go slack. If the calf kicks free within six seconds, the tie is declared invalid.

Flag Grab (Gymkhana). Four barrels are placed at opposite ends of the arena. On top of each barrel is a bucket with a flag in it. The rider must race around the outside of the barrels while moving the flag from bucket #1 to bucket #2, then moving the flag from bucket #3 to bucket #4. The cowboy or cowgirl who successfully moves both flags in the shortest amount of time is the winner.

Intermission. During intermission, funny clowns entertain the crowd.

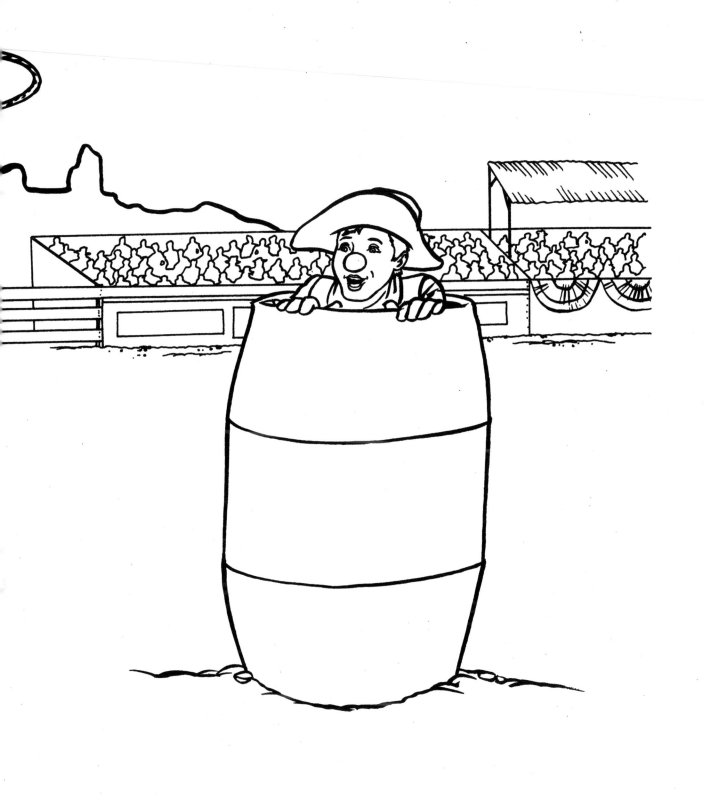

Trick Riding. These skilled equestrians specialize in performing daredevil stunts as their horses gallop around the arena.

Trick Riding. This daring rider rides with one foot on the back of two different galloping horses. Stunts like these are for experts only!

Steer Wrestling. This rugged sport requires a combination of great strength and skill. To begin, the wrestler (called a "bulldogger") catches up to the racing steer, slides off his horse and prepares to grasp the animal by the horns.

Steer Wrestling. After catching the steer, the wrestler must bring the animal to a stop or change the direction of the steer's body before throwing it to the ground. The event is over when the steer is on his side with all four legs pointing in the same direction. Steer wrestling is known as the "big man's event," because steer wrestlers are usually large and brawny, often weighing over 200 pounds!

Rodeo Champion. The contestant with the highest score wins a beautiful trophy cup and an engraved silver belt buckle.

Junior Steer Riding. The rules are the same as for regular bull riding, except young riders are allowed to use two hands. However, the rider will usually receive higher marks from the judges if he or she uses only one hand to hang on. The maximum age for contestants is usually about fifteen.

Mutton Bustin'. This young persons' contest requires children to ride a sheep out of a chute and into the rodeo arena. Like the regular cowboy bucking events, time and score count, as boys and girls cling to the sheep as hard and as long as they can.

Pig Chase. Catching a greased pig is one of the most popular and exciting rodeo events for children. First one to "bring home the bacon" wins a prize.